From Piles
To Files

Lisa Cole

Cover design by Naked Website Design

Proofreader: Thea Watson

ISBN: 9781521115084

ACKNOWLEDGMENTS

With thanks to Thea Watson and Jen Gale from www.jengale.co.uk

Table of contents

INTRODUCTION 6

IS YOUR PAPERWORK OUT OF CONTROL? 7

THE QUICK PAPERWORK DECLUTTERING METHOD 9

5 GUIDED DAYS TO SORT OUT YOUR PAPERWORK 12

PAPERWORK DAY 1: GET IT ALL TOGETHER 14

PAPERWORK DAY 2: INITIAL SORTING 16

PAPERWORK DAY 3: FILING WORK AND MONEY RELATED PAPERWORK 19

PAPERWORK DAY 4: REFERENCE PAPERS 21

PAPERWORK DAY 5: SHREDDING AND STRATEGIES 23

CONTROL STRATEGY TO STOP PAPERWORK COMING INTO YOUR HOME 25

CONTROLLING PAPERWORK QUICK REFERENCE 27

KEEPING PAPERS FOR REFERENCE 29

KEEPING ON TOP OF THINGS 30

BONUS – DECLUTTER SHELVES THE EASY WAY IN 5 MINUTES 31

DO YOU WANT TO KNOW MORE ABOUT EASY DECLUTTERING? 33

ABOUT THE AUTHOR 34

INTRODUCTION

From piles to files

I f paperwork has got the better of you and the thought of finding your passport makes you cry this is the book for you.

Can't face all of your paperwork at once? Don't worry, there is a quick decluttering method that will start to make an impact slowly and gently.

If you want to sort it out properly and get a system in place to make it easier in the future there are five days of guided paperwork decluttering, each day improving on the last and helping you create a filing system that is just for you.

With ideas for stopping the flow of paperwork into your house and an easy method for maintaining your papers this book gently guides you from piles of paperwork to files.

'I am a few minutes into reading and now crying tears of relief. I thought it would be impossible. Not now.' Clare, UK

'Just a few hours' work over 5 days and my massive piles of paper were tamed into files with everything having its own place – even a box for the pens so I never have to hunt for one again.' Arabella, UK

IS YOUR PAPERWORK OUT OF CONTROL?

Can you find important documents when you need them?

In just 5 days you could have an easy to run filing system for both your work and home life.

'I am a self confessed paperwork hater, but ignoring it doesn't make it go away... so I tried the less-stuff 5 days of de-cluttering e-course. After 5 days and about four hours work I have a simplified filing system and some good habits established to help me keep paper under control. My head feels clearer and paperwork is no longer a chore.'

You will learn

- How to identify paper you really need to keep
- How to set up an easy to use filing system for work and financial records
- How to make it easy to find those bits of paper you keep for 'one day' because they are useful
- How to set up a really simple system to keep it under control
- How to get into the habit of filing painlessly

If you follow the instructions and make some time to do this course I promise you it will work.

If you work from home, are a member of any groups, subscribe to magazines or even just get the occasional Saturday paper it is really easy to collect a huge amount of paperwork in a very short time. If you have piles of paper all over the place this method will work for you. If you have a vague filing system in place already, these 5 days will help you knock it into shape.

This book will teach you two methods of sorting out and decluttering your paperwork. There is one goal in mind – to find the right bits of paper when you need them. That is what we are working towards.

If you are short on time

The quick paperwork decluttering method shows you how to deal with your paperwork in 5 minutes a day. This is the minimal effort, no stress approach. It takes longer overall but if the thought of turning everything out repels you, this is the place to start.

Do you want to sort it out properly?

5 guided days to sort out your paperwork guides you through every day in detail and will help you sort out all of your paperwork. This requires more time but not as much as you imagine. If you take half an hour a day you will start to see some movement in the right direction pretty quickly.

At the end of the 5 days you should have your very own filing system. Once you have a structure in place for your papers you will find that the odd 5 minute here and there is all you need to keep it under control.

Decluttering paperwork is the only time I'll suggest that you get everything into one place and sort through it. The first time you do this it is unlikely to be a lot of fun but once you have worked through the daily tasks you will have a system that is easy to maintain and the overhaul won't have to be done again – unless you find that kind of thing fun!

THE QUICK PAPERWORK DECLUTTERING METHOD

This chapter gives you a strategy to start sorting your paperwork out. You will need to keep dipping into this to make it work; just spending 5 minutes a day will make a big difference.

If the very thought of filing makes you want to run away then start here. The quick paperwork decluttering method is a honed down version of the full 5 day course so it gives you an idea of things to come.

Paperwork is a clutter area which can very quickly become totally overwhelming.

Becoming overwhelmed is not the object of the game!

Be aware that you need to take this slowly.

If you want to do more than 5 things I suggest you do it in 5 minute batches.

Spend no more than 5 minutes at a time on a pile of papers then have a break.

Because we will not be tipping out boxes of letters and magazines, you will easily be able to leave the job and come back to it later.

You will need 3 boxes to sort into, or a place to make 3 new piles. This is basic sorting, there is no filing involved here, nothing needs to be put away right now.

All you need to do is take the first 5 bits of paper. They will fit into one of these categories:

1) paperwork that needs Filing

2) paperwork that needs Binning or Shredding

3) paperwork to keep for Reference

You might find it useful to have a fourth pile for things that need responding to NOW.

1) Paperwork that needs Filing is easy to spot: it will be bills, instruction manuals (unless you can easily find them online), letters from schools, contact lens prescriptions...

2) Paperwork that needs Binning or Shredding can be slightly more difficult to spot. I'm self employed so I keep records for 7 years. I love getting rid of a years' records when those 7 years are up! You probably don't need to keep information from the phone company you used 20 years ago; you definitely don't need junk mail.

3) Paperwork to keep for Reference is the hardest because it is easy to keep so much that you will not be able to find it when you need it.

Ask yourself:

- Is it about something I will never get around to?
- Is it about a place I will never go to?
- Does it bring up bad memories?
- Do I need it?
- Is it out of date?
- Can I find this information online?
- Will I ever need this bit of paper?

If it really is something that you need to keep, then it can go in the reference pile.

What will happen with this approach is that you will eventually have 3 sorted piles of paperwork.

The first pile can be filed when you have time for it; at least you know that you will be able to find the car insurance documents or the most recent gas bill in that pile. The second pile can be disposed of or recycled and the third pile can be stored.

This is a great way to start to get control of your paperwork. If you can get rid of the stuff that is clearly rubbish you are more likely to be able to find the stuff you need.

5 GUIDED DAYS TO SORT OUT YOUR PAPERWORK

This 5 day course will help you sort out your paperwork into a manageable system. The goal is at the end of the 5 days to have all the papers you need to keep filed in a way you can find them.

You should have ready

A reward: how are you going to treat yourself when you have finished this job?

A space big enough to gather all your paperwork in one place: this can be a floor, a table, even a spare bed if you have one. The important thing is that it will not be disturbed by anyone other than you in the 5 days. If this is impossible then you will need 3 medium sized cardboard boxes which you can sort into that can then be put away, or moved to the side at the end of the day.

Something to file into: this can be anything from box files to paper envelopes. Whatever you have to file into must be able to hold a reasonable amount of paper. I personally like the metal cases with hanging dividers; they are not expensive and they are supposed to be fireproof which is reassuring! Poundland often sells cheap card folders which are perfect for the job. Get lots and keep the receipts in case you want to take some back.

What your filing system looks like in the end is totally up to you. You can file into old envelopes but the easier it is to file, and the nicer your filing container, the more likely you are to do it. Avoid anything that is fiddly to open, or that explodes with papers when you undo it.

Avoid sticky drawers or hanging files that fall off the rails. Aim to use something that is smooth and easy to operate.

Plan your time

Allocate some time to do this course. Depending on how much paperwork you have to sort out expect to spend between half an hour to 3 hours (in half hour chunks) every day this week. Some days will be quicker than others.

Avoid overwhelm

It's easy to feel swamped by the enormity of the task when faced with paperwork. Go very slowly, do small bits at a time and reward yourself regularly. Make it possible for you to leave the job and have frequent breaks by not tipping out boxes of letters and magazines all over the place.

PAPERWORK DAY 1: GET IT ALL TOGETHER

Today your task is to get all your paperwork in one place.

Look for:

- Magazines
- Junk mail
- Letters
- Bills
- Receipts
- Medical records
- Minutes of meetings
- Flyers and adverts
- Brochures and catalogs
- 'Useful' bits of paper
- Lists
- Instructions
- Patterns
- Greetings cards

Go through your home and check surfaces, drawers, cupboards… gather it all up and put it all in a place which will not be disturbed for the rest of the week. If that is impossible then put it in boxes that you can move to the side away from prying hands and tripping feet.

Do you have an existing filing system in place?

If you are happy with it you can file directly into it. If it is not working for you I suggest you make new folders using larger categories. There is no need to empty all your old files out, simply go through them and check to see if there is anything in them that is in the wrong place or can be binned. Keep things that should be in folders in them because even if you decide to change your system tomorrow it will help if things are grouped together.

If you are happy with your system as it is then you are one step ahead!

When you have all the bits of paper in your home in one place, today's task is finished! Well done! The worst is over.

PAPERWORK DAY 2: INITIAL SORTING

On day 2 of the course you should have all your paperwork in one place. If you haven't done that yet you can either do it now, or see how you get on with just a fraction of your paperwork.

The method will work either way, though if you need to set up a filing system it will work better for you if you sort all the paperwork at once.

What we are going to do is put things into broad categories, which can then be split up. There is a lot to be said for the 'touch the bit of paper once' approach to filing but that will not work unless you know where the bit of paper should go.

If you have a filing system set up already leave it as it is, don't empty it all out; we will deal with it tomorrow.

You will need 3 boxes to sort into, or a place to make 3 new piles. This is basic, first level sorting: there is no filing involved here; nothing needs to be put away right now.

Allocate yourself half hour chunks of time to do this task and make sure you have a break after half an hour. It might take more than half an hour in total but don't do more than that in one go or you risk burning out.

All you need to do is take the first 5 bits of paper from the nearest pile. They will fit into one of these categories:

- Paperwork that needs Filing
- Paperwork that needs Binning or Shredding
- Paperwork to keep for Reference

If you dig up stuff that brings up unpleasant memories but you feel you have to keep it for a bit longer you can file it immediately into a 'things to forget' folder. You don't need to keep looking at it all week.

You might find it useful to have a fourth pile for things that need responding to NOW but I suggest you leave attending to them until later in the week because your head will be clearer.

Making 3 piles

1) Paperwork that needs Filing is easy to spot: it will be bills, instruction manuals (unless you can easily find them online), letters from schools, contact lens prescriptions... things relating to your health, your work, your home go in this pile.

2) Paperwork that needs Binning or Shredding can be slightly more difficult to spot. I'm self employed so I keep records for 7 years. I love getting rid of a years' records when those seven years are up! You probably don't need to keep information from the phone company you used 20 years ago; you definitely don't need junk mail!

3) Paperwork to keep for Reference is the hardest because it is easy to keep so much that you will not be able to find it when you need it. It can be anything from recipes to music manuscripts, old photos to inspirational magazine cuttings. The reference pile is for anything you want to keep that isn't related to work or money (which should go into the first filing pile).

Ask yourself:

- Is it about something I will never get around to?
- Is it about a place I will never go to?
- Does it bring up bad memories?
- Do I need it?
- Is it out of date?
- Can I find this information online?
- Will I ever need this bit of paper?

If it really is something that you need to keep, then it can go in the reference pile.

What will happen with this approach is that you will eventually have 3 sorted piles or boxes of paperwork.

You can dip in and out of this task through the day or you can tackle it in larger, half hour chunks. You will need to concentrate so make sure you take frequent breaks.

PAPERWORK DAY 3: FILING WORK AND MONEY RELATED PAPERWORK

After yesterday, you should have 3 piles or boxes of papers. If you haven't done this you will need to before you go onto the next step, which is sorting out the filing pile.

Today you will be filing into something, so you will need those folders, files or boxes to be ready.

Sorting out the pile of papers to be filed

The filing pile should be stuff that is relevant to money or work; if you find things that you are keeping for personal reasons, recipes, newspaper clippings etc. they should go into the reference pile.

A trap that a lot of people fall into when they are setting up a filing system is that they make the files too specific. I don't have a file just for car insurance, I have one for 'car stuff' which includes insurance, tax, receipts from the mechanic, my drivers license, local parking permit stuff, and also my spare keys just in case. I know that if I need to find anything related to my car, it will be in that file.

The way to set up this sort of broad system is to take the first bit of paper from the filing pile or box. What is it? Your contact lens prescription? That is a medical thing and would go under 'health' or 'medical' or any other broad category that makes sense to you.

Grab the first bit of paper, decide what it is, mark a folder for it and file it.

Keep doing this and work your way through the pile. If you come across something tricky, put it to the bottom of the file and deal with it at the end.

As you work through your paperwork you may find that some folders will need to be merged into one, or you may see that a folder really needs to be split.

Take it slowly, take frequent breaks!

Today is just about that one pile so once that is done take a break and come back to it tomorrow.

Some categories I have which may help you decide are:

- Car stuff
- Utilities (gas, electricity, water rates and council tax)
- Phone (broadband and mobile)
- Letters from school/work
- Health (glasses prescription)
- Important (passports and birth certificates)
- Benefits
- Bank statements
- Savings (details of premium bonds because I live in hope!)
- Receipts

As you go through you might find some things that should be in the bin or shred pile too!

PAPERWORK DAY 4: REFERENCE PAPERS

What sort of things are you keeping for reference? As you sort out this pile go through the checklist again.

Ask yourself:

- Is it about something I will never get around to?
- Is it about a place I will never go to?
- Does it bring up bad memories?
- Do I need it?
- Is it out of date?
- Can I find this information online?
- Will I ever need this bit of paper?

If you find things that bring up unhappy memories or that you don't want to think about right now and cannot throw away it's fine to just make a new folder for them and let them sit there until you feel strong enough to deal with them. It's better to have them out of sight than nagging you all the time.

If the first bit of paper you pick up passes all the tests and you really want to keep it then you need to find a broad category for it.

Categories might include:

- Hobbies (if you have hundreds this might need breaking down further but you can do that later)
- Images you like
- Inspirations
- Recipes
- Old birthday and Christmas cards (ask yourself why you are keeping them first, you might be able to let them go)
- Memorabilia from great days out
- Sheet music

You know how this works now! Pick up a bit of paper, judge it and if it passes assign it a folder with a category.

You will need to concentrate so make sure you have frequent breaks! At the end of today your reference pile should be sorted!

Did you have an 'Urgent' pile from earlier this week? If so you could spend just 5 minutes working through that. See what you can get done in that time.

Remember, it's really important to take frequent breaks, get away from the papers, go and have a cup of tea, stare at some clouds, anything to stop you becoming overwhelmed.

If you get stuck, look at the bit of paper and ask yourself what category it is in. This will be personal to everyone but the broad category should be pretty clear and that is the file it should go into.

PAPERWORK DAY 5: SHREDDING AND STRATEGIES

Congratulations! You made it to the last day!

What an enormous achievement it is to have sorted out your paperwork. If there are still bits left to do you can go back and revisit the previous chapters. It's fine if it takes you longer than 5 days to sort it all out; every day you spend 5 minutes on it is a move forward. If you have rooms full of paperwork this method works, just stick with it.

You should have 2 main filing systems now – one for 'work and money' type things filled with broad categories and another for 'personal' reference type things.

You should have a big pile of paperwork left: all the junk! Now is the day to get rid of it. Some of it could be recycled but you might want to shred or burn other bits of it. That's up to you. Today is the day to clear it all out.

Try not to work for more than half an hour at a time, you are more likely to succeed at this task quickly if you take breaks!

Control strategy to avoid messing it all up again

When you have organised your filing you will need a system in place to make sure it doesn't get out of hand again.

I use the dumping ground method.

You need one central location to put paperwork in as it comes in. I have a wooden box on my desk. Everything that comes into the house that isn't clearly immediately destined for the recycle bin goes in here. When the box is full I go through the stages to sort it out.

3 piles of paper:

Pile 1 – paperwork that needs Filing

Pile 2 – paperwork that needs Binning or Shredding

Pile 3 – paperwork to keep for Reference

Sometimes I make a fourth pile for things that need dealing with right now. It takes me well under half an hour a month to keep it all under control now.

CONTROL STRATEGY TO STOP PAPERWORK COMING INTO YOUR HOME

Op the junk mail. If you are in the UK you can register with the Mail Preference Service. This is free and will remove your name and address from industry mailing lists. Royal Mail have a form you can fill in to stop the door to door junk mail your postman brings too.

The United States of America Government site has a list of ways to opt-out of junk mail.

In Australia you can opt out at the Association for Data-Driven Marketing and Advertising.

Register for online bills and statements. You will be able to see them when you log into your account and print them if you really need to. You can print from the library if you don't have a printer at home.

If you are storing instruction manuals see if you can get them online instead. It is often easier to search for specific problems online too. Search by the appliance number if you can find it.

Pinterest is a great way to store ideas for craft projects and recipes. You can organise your own boards by topics and add images and links you find inspiring.

Online storage sites such as <u>Evernote</u> are great for keeping important notes organised. You can add reminder dates too.

So that is it. I hope you have had a wonderful week and feel amazing looking at your organised paperwork right now. Life does get in the way of sorting things out so if you need more time, take it. You can do it! I did!

CONTROLLING PAPERWORK QUICK REFERENCE

Initial sorting

1) Paperwork that needs Filing: bills, instruction manuals (unless you can easily find them online), letters from schools, contact lens prescriptions... things relating to your health, your work, your home.

2) Paperwork that needs Binning or Shredding: junk mail, menus, flyers, records over 7 years old.

3) Paperwork to keep for Reference: recipes, music manuscripts, old photos, magazine cuttings, anything you want to keep that isn't related to work or money (which should go into the first filing pile).

Designing a filing system

Remember broad categories are easier.

Sample categories for filing:

- Car stuff
- Utilities (gas, electricity, water rates and council tax)
- Phone (broadband and mobile)
- Letters from school
- Health (glasses prescription)
- Important (passports and birth certificates)

- Benefits (tax credits send you huge amounts of paperwork!)
- Bank statements
- Savings (details of premium bonds because I live in hope!)
- Receipts

KEEPING PAPERS FOR REFERENCE

Do I need to keep it? Checklist:

- Is it about something I will never get around to?
- Is it about a place I will never go to?
- Does it bring up bad memories?
- Do I need it?
- Is it out of date?
- Can I find this information online?
- Will I ever need this bit of paper?

KEEPING ON TOP OF THINGS

The dumping ground method.

As it comes into the house put paperwork in one place.

Regularly (once a month) sort into 3 piles of paper for refiling:

Pile 1 – paperwork that needs Filing

Pile 2 – paperwork that needs Binning or Shredding

Pile 3 – paperwork to keep for Reference

Make a fourth pile for things to deal with urgently if required.

Remember to take frequent breaks and take it slowly. If you come across something that brings up bad memories be kind to yourself and file it in a 'forget' folder if it can't be thrown out now.

If you have found this approach fun and feel you need to declutter other areas in your home or work please visit www.less-stuff.co.uk

Less-stuff is all about decluttering for people who love stuff. We are not minimalists or hoarders and we don't ever purge or blitz our belongings. Learn the decluttering habits that will make life easier for you and keep your clutter under control.

BONUS – DECLUTTER SHELVES THE EASY WAY IN 5 MINUTES

This is a sample of the type of decluttering guide used on www.less-stuff.co.uk. There are many different guides that cover everything from email to underwear.

Less-stuff is not about chucking everything out and leading a minimalistic lifestyle, it's about choosing with intent the things you keep around you. If everyone else around you thinks something is hideous, but it means somethi to you, has good memories and makes you happy then keep it!

For everything else, here is a way to identify quickly what you don't need in your life.

Today, we are going to tackle one shelf or surface in your home. It can be in any room but as an easy start, just choose the one nearest to you.

Look at the clutter on it and ask yourself:

- Do I use it?

- Do I like it?

- Is it a part of something else I lost a long time ago?

- Is it broken?

- Should it be there?

- Have I got more than one of them?

- Will I ever use it?

- Is it ugly?

- Is it something you mean to finish but probably won't?

- Is it something you are keeping because it was a gift but you don't like it?

If, on your way, you find broken things then throw them away or recycle them. You can count them in your 5 things too if you like.

The whole point of this is to get your home full of usable things that you like and that make you feel good.

If your shelves are full of things that make you very happy then keep them. If they don't make you happy then why have them in your house?

Just 5 minutes for 5 things. It's easy.

Choose small, not expensive, obvious things for today's declutter.

DO YOU WANT TO KNOW MORE ABOUT EASY DECLUTTERING?

Make it easy for yourself to declutter daily in less than 5 minutes by following the step by step instructions here www.less-stuff.co.uk/start-here/

Sign up to the less-stuff mailing list for freebies and downloads that will help you declutter easily and live a simpler life.

ABOUT THE AUTHOR

Lisa Cole lives in Bristol with her teenage son and too many cats. Lisa believes that it's fine to have stuff, but it's good to be able to find it when you need it. On her website www.less-stuff.co.uk she shares ideas and strategies that help people live easier lives, with less clutter. It's decluttering for real people. She is not a minimalist or a guru.

Milton Keynes UK
Ingram Content Group UK Ltd.
UKHW011958211223
434792UK00004B/280